بسم الله الرحمن الرحيم

In the name of Allah
The Most Merciful, the Most Kind.

Do you think that We created you
Without purpose and that you
Would not be returning to Us?

- Quran 23:115

RETURNING

Kheir Publications
www.thekheir.com

In loving memory of

Lunnette Blair

Contact info:

Email – abdulmalik.skt786@gmail.com

Facebook – Abdul Malik

Instagram – Abdulmalik.86

KHEiR PUBLICATIONS

www.thekheir.com

ISBN-13: 978-1999843205
ISBN-10: 1999843207

Illustrated by – Ruqayyah Forbes
Edits by – Zaynab Heath
Cover art by – Jesh_designs

Please pray for us all.

RETURNING

THE FLOWER

This Love

This poetry is not from me.
It is something that fills me
And spills out when I am filled.
Something that stills me
And sings out when I am stilled.

This poetry is not from me
But for me...
A gift
That only feels as though
it's been fulfilled
When I share it...
with you.

Content

Introduction

We know each other well, you and I. Deep down in the core of our souls, we are connected like individual links of a chain that interlock as part of a whole.

We have been apart for a long time and judging by the fact that you are here, I can safely assume that you have survived the journey thus far.

I have been seeking cognisance. Searching this ever changing terrain for knowledge that will reconnect us with the divine.

A knowledge that is with the flowers. Attracting the seeker to mercy and kindness with a silent but fragrant call. Patiently pushing through darkness and hardship in order to blossom and present the beauty of its source.

The seeker of knowledge is like the bee, waiting for the flower to unfasten so that it may take from its goodness and turn it into sweetness and healing for the world.

One day the bee will become the flower just as the seeker becomes the sought.
This is the returning from the flower.

The Flower

I once asked the flower:

"What is the purpose of all this?"

It replied:

"To open up and share love with all."

The Union

I cannot remember the last time my
Heart screamed this loudly in
Recognition of the known.

This is not a uniting.
This is a reuniting
Of what was once together.
And then alone.
Then found,
Tied, sewn and grown.

I know you, so remember me.

Close your eyes,
Open your mind,
Then
Take a dive into this river,
And learn to swim like that.

The water is ruff sometimes.
Mostly calm.
But always leads to the ocean.

This is the union

The beauty of this morning's light,
Radiates upon the start of a fresh journey.
One day my physical
Will not be visible to you,
So let us cherish the now
That we may recognise each other then.

The union of souls that intertwine
Like two cascading plaits of rope,
Stretching into the far distance of forever.

Like the union between
The ribs and the heart
And
The one between
The rose and the rain.
The union of
You and I
Again.

Root

Though we may not always see the root,
We come to know its spirit through
The flowers it encourages to blossom.

The Flower & The Root

"I love you"
Heard the flower from the root
As it spoke in truth.

"Though we grow in two directions
There is still a fine connection
Between you and I.
Seen and the unseen.
Earth and sky.

The miner digging for diamonds
And the one who rose high towards the heavens,
Seeking the pleasant presence of the sun.

In truth,
I could never leave you, I need you.
Knowledge is but light and I concede to
Asking for a piece of this light so I can feed you.
That's how the seed grew.

Knowledge eliminates the darkest regions.
So keep growing,
An I'll keep you in duas this season.

Ease showing,
Breeze blowing even more this year
But don't synthesis the thoughts of fear,
Though you may not see me,

I support you,

I

Am always near,
Powered by the force of prayer.
Deep.. In truth,
You flower, I root.
Speaking through our vine connection,
Hoping that this vibe will set in...
Give thanks for the finer blessings.
Aspire to the highest heavens.
Reply to the divine with reverence.
A presence you can define in seconds...
...**Love**.

And the summer's air is near
So beware of the gardener
Who seeks to pick an discard ya.

There's beauty in the rain and in
You.

So even when the clouds show,
Know this is a time of growth.

Moving through the pain.

Your fragrant vibrations seeping in loads.
It seems,
The more you open up, the deeper I grow,
In my own direction.
A reflection of your sublime complexion.
Seen and the unseen
Stay connected through a vine subjected
To truth:

"Everything returns to where it came.
What is two becomes one a-gain."

"We are connected with love," says the flower in
reply.
"I love you, you love I."

Share

Let me take of what you
carry, so you can hold the
stuff of cure.

Trust

There are no coincidences.

Allah's plan is the best of all.

Story Of A Brief Encounter

The weather, it snowed.
The breeze, it blew.
The night, was calm.
The beauty, exposed.

Their baby was there,
No sound did he cry.
He wasn't alone.
The angel arrived.

The eyes, they cried.
The smiles, they came.
The warmth was there,
The heart it glowed.

Their baby was there,
No sound did he cry.
He wasn't alone,
The angel beside.

The mother was there,
The father was too.
Grandparents, aunties,
uncles and nephews.

Their baby was there,
No sound did he cry.
He wasn't alone,
The angel and I.

The sweetest of songs of hope they'd sing.
Each greeting of folk, more cope they'd bring.
His hair was hers, his feet was his.
His heart, in ours always it lives.

A fighter, a seeker, the laughter, the love,
The spirit, the brains, the realist of us.

He didn't live long, so short was his time.
The soul lives on, the body it dies.

There baby was there,
No sound did he cry,
He isn't alone
With angels he flies.

The snow came for days,
Then slowly change to rain.
In heat it changed again.
Then back to where it came.

Inna lillahi wa inna ilayhi rajioon
(From Him we come and to Him
We are returning.)

Patience

Be patient my friend...
...Then...
...Be persistent
In your patience...
...All the way....
...To …
The End.

It's Not Here

I have stopped searching for it here.
Paradise.
It is,
With no man
Nor woman,
Nor country
Or taste.
No feeling or sensation of this temporary state.

Do not tempt me with your temptation.
That kindles,
Then burns.
Then is gone with the briskness of the blink.
The once sweet now ever bitter.

I will wait.
No pain is permanent here.
For there is glad tidings for patient beings.

Those most hungry today,
Will be the most full when that long, hard
Day of judging comes.

Spring always follows winter.
The flower in its dormancy
Hopes to be raised
And reunited
With the rays that brought it to life.
Freedom is only there.
Not here
Nor any land you are in.
Illusion is partnered with this world,
So distance my heart from any of its claims
Or its blames
And keep me among the humble
Until I leave.
Alone.
With only my deeds to show.
When my creed is probed,
Dreams are broke
And reality is.
Oh Allah, forgive me for my sins
My shortcomings
And my whims.
Let not my actions be just for the sake of
action.
In that state indeed I am away from you.
My Lord
Help me to remember You.

When The Heart Is Broken

When the heart is broken.
The angels say,
"Return to Allah, remember Allah"
Whilst the Shayateen says,
"Rebel."

May Allah grant us the best of company,

Outer and inner,

Seen and unseen.

Ameen.

Alone

Say to the lonely:

"You are never alone."

Light

I Pray Allah protects you
And keeps your spirits high.
When days are feeling dull and grey
And clouds blot out the sky.
Just know there is a ray of light
That seeks to light the world.
To bring a smile to all it reach
And gather hearts in love.
That light is always shining
No matter they say nor do.
That light it grew the garden
That garden grew and grew.
I ask the one who made that light
To keep your spirit high,
As your spirit is a mercy
Like the light that lights the sky.

Struggle

Struggling through the darkness,

I heard you say...

Keep pushing,

Things will get better.

It's Temporary

"One thing I've learnt about this world,"

He said.

"All its pleasures and its pains are

Temporary."

...

"Give thanks for what you have

And what you've had."

Fill

Fill your heart

With the kind of love

That never dies.

Accepting

"Stay with the flow of the breeze,"
He whispered.

"Otherwise I fear you will break

Beyond repair."

Mother

He Asked:

"When was the last time

You sat with your mother?

There's healing in her pleasure.

Her pleasure is a home.

So please her

And never underestimate

The value of small good
Deeds."

I Love You

I am not ashamed to
Say I love you
In all that I do.

The Soul Enters

The soul penetrates the womb and enters the
Foetus just as the drop of rain penetrates the
Earth and enters the seed.

Heart

Amidst the muscles that moaned daily

And back bones that complained daily

Of the excess weight they were made to
Bravely embrace.

There was a heart that was in love with me,

That kept my heart company

In the depths of the darkness and strange.

Every beat that it spoke

Would tell me that it's close

Of love and of hope it kept telling me.

And there's no need to fear

My love will always be there.

We're as close as two hearts could ever be.

Thank you

Paradise lies
Beneath your feet,
So love and prayers
For you we seek.

Return

Listen closely...

Look closely...

His nature.

It's among

The most beautiful

Poetry

Of All...

Return...

Reconnect...

Reflecting

Beginning
In your remembrance.
I am one with the universe.
The universe is one within me.
Bowing as a slave shows reverence
To the king.

Prostrating.
I am less than an atom of dust,
On the floor of your court.
And
Your dominion is vastness and truth.
Guide me onto you,
As you unto me are a guide.

Returning
As you unto me are guiding,
Guide me onto you.
Your dominion is vastness and truth.
And
On the floor of your court,
I am less than an atom of dust,

Prostrating
To the King.
Bowing as a slave shows reverence.

The universe is one within me.
I am one with the universe,
In your remembrance.
Let my ending be,
Alhamdulillah.

Seeking

I was looking for love.
My teacher told me that love
Cannot hide.
It shows its signs
Clear to us,
Right here for us to find.
It's obvious, the problem is...
Us...
We're blind.
Instead of seeing with the heart,
We're seeking with the eyes.

Unravel

Unravel the veils of your heart.
Layer by layer.
Until your essence is in the presence of its beat.
Then let actions be the words to its vibration.
Enlightening the souls of those you meet.

Those who seek to dance too.
Those seeking love.
Those seeking life.
Those seeking to paint, think, teach and speak.
Those seeking the deep beyond,
Hoping to reach the long,
Lost treasure of content.

And we were sent
To peel away the layers of the heart.
Veil by veil,
Until our essence is in the pleasant of its fruit.
Become the proof.
And let the heart be a cure for the dying.

The internal becomes external.
Conceal not what you feel.
Addressing what is inner
And expressing what is real.

Until your being becomes a beacon,
From a whisper no longer hoarse.
Asking how can one feel fear when one's
connected to the source.

Veils

"What are the veils of the heart?"
I asked.

"Ego and whimsical desires."
He answered.

"And its fruit?"
"Presents with God."

Chakra

The heart chakra shines

The Brightest.

Polish it often

So that it may light the way.

How is it polished?

By forgiving

And

Seeking forgiveness...

. . . .

Please forgive me.

Emit

Emit love.

Love will return.

Eyes Of Love

Look with the eyes of love

And beauty

Becomes everywhere apparent.

Love Time

If we are not using our time

To spread love,

We are wasting time.

A Gift

He Said,
"Here, take this for your journey,
Use it.
Never lose it.
It will take you where you want to
go."

Then he gave me a smile.

Smile

He said :
"I take my smiling faces very seriously.
The energy of a smile with sincerity,
Brings serenity to the heart, it's a remedy.

You see clemency is a trait of the heavenly."
Then he got deeper in song and in melody.

He said:
"What is in the heart will eventually
Manifest on the tongue.
So it's not unusual
For beautiful people
To speak only beautiful things,
Even when they are wronged.

The Prophet Muhammad sallalahu alayhi
Wa salam proclaims,
The heart is a container,
Meaning:
It can only pour forth what it contains.

The Smile is
The cloud that forms
And springs forth water
As falling rain.
And with the sun's warmth,
Spring sprung forth
And brought us grain
So we could graze.
Then
From the hearts hard as rocks,
Springs sprung forth.
It's like the mind that pops open and
Springs some thoughts into existence,
Something so pure and realistic,
It brings some cure to the afflicted
And flings us forward into upliftment.

I've never been so sure
That when someone's gifted,
Peace,
Real peace,
It can link us all...

...To the omnipotent..."

He said : "I was in denial
But the signs are in a smile."

He paused.

I thought...
I said: "Sing some more."

He said:
"To have positivity is to acknowledge inner
belief. It's to always have the feeling that you
could.

Within positivity there is.....
.....love.....

...So smile..."

I said "What if am not feeling good?
Or I feel it,
But the one who is receiving doesn't?
Or am grieving,
And the stuff that am concealing's tough,
And unappealing,
From the dealings of a season's rough."

He smiled for a while
And said: "Just keep it up.
Keep a smile
Even if the heart is bleeding blood.

Within a smile there's a sign for the believing.
Within a smile there is healing and relief for us."

Then he changes and says this:

"Never arrange to stay close,
To those
Enraged volcanoes,
Engaged with spewing great loads
Of rocks an flames thrown
Out of anger.

It's contagious,
The smile is a sign of the courageous.

That smile on your face is a light for my heart
Then
That light in my heart puts a smile on my face.

Small gestures affect hearts in large ways.
So smile...

Just smile.
Is it not the arrival
Of the butterfly's recital
That causes the tide to tidal?

Wave goodbye to the idle
And ascribe to the smile.
If inside you is vile,
I prescribe you the smile.
If you want beauty to find you
Advice is to smile,
If you move with a style
Then your duty's to smile.

Have love for all,
I know I do.
Life's too short to be spiteful.
To be caught in a cycle of
Scorn
Is to spiral.

A smile could change a world.
A smile can change the world.

It ripples the outside
From the universe that's inside you.
Crippling doubt, pride
Or any plight we're confined to.
The issue is our time,
It's final,
So it's vital,
We make the ego our rival
An be the first to just smile."

He said:
"I take my smiling faces very seriously.
Where there's teeth with sincerity,
There is peace and serenity
There is ease for the heart,
A relief from the harsh."...
So smile.

Stranded

I found myself...
Stranded.
Waiting for you to arrive.

Root

In its love,
The root nurtures
Even the furthest of branches.

The Bird & The Tree

The old tree had felt it all
Through summers and winters past.
The trees that rise and those that fall,

Some victim to the axe.
The animals would come from far to seek

His cooling shade.
But man had made a plan for him
As paper, fuel and grave.
The tree he knew but he stayed true

Accepting of his fate.
The time will come when he'll become

A table for man's plate.

Until a day there came a bird,
Wings wiping through the breeze.
It saw the tree an felt at ease,
So sat among his leaves.
It sang a song of beauty there,

One heavenly and sweet.

The other birds felt obsolete,
As they could only tweet.
It sang a tune of travels wide
And freedoms in the skies.
Of how it found its heart in that
Whose roots had deeply dived.
The tree would flower fruits and shade,
The bird would chirp a cure.
The people came in herds of awe
To gaze at their amour.
The seasons changed, the tree became,
More withered, wilt and froze.
So sent the bird away to find some
Shelter from the cold.
It didn't want to turn from him,
It sensed their love was tight.
It promised a return in spring with
Songs of summer light.
With that it left the tree alone
But home was here for sure.
It flew away, he hoped some day
It'd sing for him some more.

Punishment

The worst punishment for the lover

Is to be distant from the beloved.

Humility

Only when the seed is split
Can new life begin to flourish
And expose itself through the
Fresh fissures that have made
Themselves known.

Here I am: broken, hoping to be
grown.

For behind the seed's hard
Exterior is the flower,

Waiting to return home.

Rain

Never complain when it's raining loads.

Plants love rain,

Rain brings growth.

Grow

Grow

Through all the mess

And all the dirt.

Grow.

The most beautiful buds

Bloom

From the darkest of places.

The Bee

They're asking me:

"How does man
Come to find Islam
In these times?"

My reply:

"Ask the bee
How it finds it's way
Back to the hive."

Muhammad

Muhammad.

I hear his name

And

Love rushes

To my heart. (pbuh)

Bridge

Praise be to He
Who creates a bridge for
Hearts to meet.
A bridge not composed of material
But....
Feel how strong it is in being.

Not concerned with distance,
It reaches all points of the universe,
Beyond the beyond and back.

Nor concerned with time,
It connects my heart with yours.
In all your states.
Then, now and then.

I ask Allah to bless you.
Instantly you ask the same,
And more,
For me,
A cure.
Before.. we were...

Born,
You called Allah to build this bridge
In order for hearts to talk with yours
And meet and seek a piece of peace.
Your peace,
The purest of the pure.
The core,
The source,
The first light.
A beacon for the seekers of Allah.
The warner and bringer of glad tidings,
The teacher of salah.
Ya Mustafa,
Habibullah.
Healer of all terrains.
The ocean of all oceans,
Mountain of all mountains

The bridge between our hearts
Is one that's felt and never seen
It's built by
Sending peace upon
Muhammad Al Ameen.

Cure?

I asked:
"What can I do to cure this sore and sick soul?"

He replied:
"Simply follow the path of the beloved.
Praise the beauty of the beloved."

Action

Let actions be the words for the heart.
Lips remain absent
And words reserved for dua.

Traverse to Allah.
Know that you're special,
Then learn that you were from the
start.

Order

Out of the chaos, He makes order.
The same order that prevents the
Moon from crashing into the earth,
As it steadily orbits the sun.
Wading through seasons, breathing,
Closer, then farther from the light.
Always sincere, circular, cooler, warmer.
Always in motion, devoted.

Even an atom's weight negates our position.
Negative and positive in balance.
Protons, steadily circulate the nucleus.
And as usual
The chaos is brought into order of the neutral.
A truthful vibration, creation, precise, calm.

To bring life to the heart and through love of Allah
People circulate the Kaba.
Humans, being, believing,
Hearts, seeing,
Ascending through the heavens as they go.
Wading through their seasons, breathing, easing,
Witnessing the closeness of the truth.
Sincere and always in motion.
Balanced.
And with the grain of the universe.

Pace

A friend told me to trust the taste
And grace
Of your own pace.
Because in a state of rush and
haste,
We tend to make mistakes.

Sister Of Death

I see you in the evening.
Under the moon and stars.
Under the sky.
Today, I long to see you tonight.

I love you,
But I have feared your sister.
Knowing one day I will meet her.
And she will take away my breath.
One day.
And we shall be together
Until I am again, awakened.

Travellers

We are travellers
On the road to Allah,
On a road built by Allah,
Sign posted by Allah,
Lit by his Rasool
Allah.
With directions that point to Jannah.

Provided we follow this light
We might sight the chance to reach
This destination.
A test of patience

In which, I pray I don't fall asleep
Or take a wrong turn
Or
Reverse
Or stay distracted by the sheep.
My brothers and sisters
Please help me stay awake.

This vessel I take
I must keep prestige.
So we read the map
To orient
faith.
To remind of where we came,
Of our return.

Although time is essential,
This is not a race.
So I move at a leisurely pace,
Taking in the beauty
Of the ever-changing scenery.

Sometimes warm, sometimes cold
But always on the road,
Until its time to return home.
Until its time to return to Allah.

Root

He said:
"When the root is rotten
The tree struggles to
Grow prosperous.
Look after your root
And feed it only goodness."

Al Kamal Wal Jamal

The Perfection and Beauty

Al Kamal wal Jamal
Every praiseworthy attribute perfected
Within your outer and inner dimensions.

The symmetry of heaven and earth.

The harmony of equality.
The order in the chaos.
Lips are cooled by the tender kiss of the
Words that supplicate your name.

Peace be upon you who
Made the wealthy see the wealth in being
Poor and the poor see pleasure in the
Decree.
We desire only what you desire to acquire.

You are the cure for the sore and sick soul.
The beloved of the Beloved.

You are humanity,
Shrouded in astounding beauty.
The celestial and terrestrial communities
Sing your eulogy
In unity.

Peace be upon you

Rasool ur-Rahmah.
Your lovers wear their hearts on their sleeve

In hope you will hold their hands.

Allah has created no deeper ocean.

There is no mountain with more humility
Nor devotee with more devotion.
No lover more extreme in love.
Blessed is your love and your lovers.
Forever.

O Allah! Give reward to our leader
Muhammad.

A reward that brings healing to the world.
Ameen.

Sacrifice

What is love without
Sacrifice for the beloved?

Some claim love but
Love sleep more than to be
With the beloved.
Or love to eat more than to
Be with the beloved.
Or speak of other than the
beloved.
Or to seek other than the
beloved.

Love that doesn't reach the
Limbs, can this be labelled
Love complete?
When apart does the heart
Weep?
Asking of when next
The lover and beloved will
Meet?

What better inspiration is
There than love?
And what better motivator?
When I fall out of it,
I take my time to fall back
Into its crater.
With its creator.
Without it humanity wavers.
Some say that fear is the best
Of motivators.
With this I disagree.
Except fear of disappointing
The instigator
Of love and its favour.
The way of love is the way of
The aviator,

Flying towards

The object of its love.

Letting the self disappear

We begin to sleep like the beloved,

Eat like the beloved,

Speak like the beloved,

Weep like the beloved,

Seek the beloved.

Love like the beloved loves.

Fly towards the beloved

And see how the lover and beloved
become one.

Home

"Where are we going?"

"Home.

We have been away for

Far too long..."

Meet Me In The Garden

Meet me in the garden,
The one where rivers flow.
Of milk and honey,
When we're done
I pray that's where we'll go.

There's one who sees our struggles.
From grief there is relief.
The angels they will meet us,
Greeting with songs of peace.

He sent His final messenger
Who taught us not to fear.
He left us these directions
On how to get us there.

Be good to all people,
Even those who vex.
Hold patience and forgiveness
As keys to your success.

An attitude of gratitude
Will help the hearts stay pure.
Be nice to both your parents
And strive to feed the poor.

What you love for you,
Try to love for others too.
Be fair in all your dealings,
Neither selfish or askew.

A smile is seen as charity,
Be respecting of the old.
Pay a visit to the sick and ill,
Show neighbours warmth not cold.

Being truthful in all circumstances,
Speaking good or keeping hush.
Will keep you out of many harms
And make you one of trust.

Waste not a speck of food
And water, not a drop.
Their value more than diamonds
Or any precious rock.

Be gentle with your spouse.
To kids show loving care.
Be kind to animals and plants
And you'll soon be there.

Be careful of desire.
Those endless wants and whims.
That lead us to temptation,
That bring the limbs to sins.

And the prayer is essential,
The central for all good.
It keeps us in God's pleasure.
Increasing one in love.

If happiness is what you seek
In these actions invest.
They'll connect us with the best of all
In this life and the next.

They'll lead us to the garden,
The one where rivers flow.
Of milk and honey,
When where done,
I pray that's where we'll go.

Be

He said:

"It only takes one flower
To make the whole bush beautiful.

BE THE FLOWER."

الحمد لله

Praise be to Allah